the
Prosecco
cookbook

PROSECCO COCKTAILS, CAKES, DINNERS & DESSERTS

 CookNation

the Prosecco cookbook
PROSECCO COCKTAILS, CAKES, DINNERS & DESSERTS

ISBN 978-1-912155-73-6

Printed and bound in Great Britain by TJ International Ltd. Padstow

Disclaimer

CONTENTS

Sweet Food   41

Cocktails   71

You May Also Enjoy...   95

Prosecco

Cooking just got glamourous!

Prosecco has become the UK's latest & greatest love affair: with Brits consuming more than 36% of all the Prosecco wine produced last year – that's 8.3 million cases in total, while in the U.S. sales are increasing rapidly with 4.2 million cases. And why not? Prosecco is better value than it's French 'cousin' Champagne - you can buy a great bottle of Prosecco for the price of a cheap bottle of champagne making it not only affordable to drink but also the perfect ingredient for cooking.

Prosecco is perfect for any occasion, be it birthday celebrations, picnics in the park or a midweek evening treat after a hard day at work. It compliments anything and now you can include this tasty tipple as the perfect new ingredient in your cooking. Suddenly the sound of popping bottles doesn't just mean there's a party happening... it can lead to some delicious results in the kitchen too: from creative cocktails & canapés to juicy chicken dinners it's time to take your Prosecco obsession into a new dimension with our delicious collection of Prosecco recipes.

A brief history of Prosecco

Prosecco is Italy's most popular & famous sparkling wine. For many years it was regarded as a poor relation to French Champagne mainly due to the fact that much of the Prosecco available wasn't of a good enough quality. However fine Proseccos have become more widely available and it now runs neck and neck with Champagne for popularity.

The name Prosecco comes from the Italian village of Prosecco where the grape originated from. Whilst the first known mention of the name "Prosecco" is attributed to the Englishman Fynes Moryson, who, visited the north of Italy in

1593, most famously the poet Aureliano Acanti wrote in 1754 "..and now I would like to wet my mouth with that Prosecco with its apple bouquet".

In the 18th century cultivation of Glera (the grape from which Prosecco comes) expanded throughout the hills of Veneto and Friuli. Production then spread to the neighbouring lower lying areas and this is where the Prosecco we know today was first produced at the beginning of the 20th century thanks to the introduction of new fermentation techniques.

Up until the 1960s, Prosecco was generally rather sweet and comparable to the Asti wine produced in Piedmont. Since then production technologies have changed to create the high-quality Prosecco produced today.
There are now 8159 wine estates and 269 sparkling wine producers and with Prosecco recently granted 'Controlled Designation of Origin' status the quality of the most famous Italian sparkling wine in the world is guaranteed.

We hope you enjoy our fabulous Prosecco recipes and get even more thrills from cooking....and Prosecco.

About CookNation

CookNation is the leading publisher of innovative and practical recipe books for the modern, health conscious cook.

CookNation titles bring together delicious, easy and practical recipes with their unique no nonsense approach - making cooking for diets and healthy eating fast, simple and fun. With a range of #1 best-selling titles - from the innovative 'Skinny' calorie-counted series, to the 5:2 Diet Recipes collection - CookNation recipe books prove that 'Diet' can still mean 'Delicious'!

To browse all CookNation's recipe books visit www.bellmackenzie.com

 **CookNation**

Prosecco Savoury Recipes

Prosecco Chicken

Ingredients

- **2 tbsp olive oil**
- **3 tbsp plain flour**
- **Salt & pepper**
- **1 tbsp orange zest**
- **1.35kg/3lb chicken, quartered**
- **150g/5oz pancetta, diced**
- **12 shallots, peeled & halved**
- **1 red chilli, seeded and finely chopped**
- **2 tsp rosemary, chopped**
- **1 bottle Prosecco**
- **Fresh rosemary sprigs, to garnish**

Method

1 Heat the olive oil in a large pan. Season the flour with salt, pepper and orange zest, then toss the chicken pieces in the flour mix until they're thoroughly coated.

2 Brown the coated chicken pieces in the pan, skin-side down, in batches if necessary. Transfer the chicken to a plate.

3 Throw the pancetta into the pan and cook until crisp. Reduce the heat. Add the shallots, chilli and rosemary and sauté for about 5 minutes.

4 Return the chicken to the pan. Pour the Prosecco over the top and simmer for 25 -30 minutes, until the sauce becomes syrupy and the chicken is all thoroughly cooked.

5 Season with salt and pepper and serve garnished with sprigs of fresh rosemary.

Enjoy with salad, and a fresh glass of Prosecco!

Prosecco & Prawn Risotto

Ingredients

- 1kg/2¼lb king prawns
- 1lt/4 cups stock
- 100g/3½oz unsalted butter
- Salt & pepper

- 1 onion, peeled and finely chopped
- 350g/12oz risotto rice
- 250ml/1 cup Prosecco

Method

1 Clean and shell the prawns.

2 In a frying pan melt about a third of the butter until it begins to bubble. Add the prawns and sauté for two minutes. Season and remove from the heat.

3 In a different frying pan, melt the remaining butter and fry the onion until soft. Add the rice and cook for a minute or two, stirring.

4 Pour in the Prosecco and cook, stirring constantly until it begins to reduce. Ladle in the hot stock, adding more as soon as it's absorbed. Repeat for about 20 minutes or until the rice is al dente.

5 Stir in the prawns and cook until pink and piping hot. Taste and adjust the seasoning and stock if necessary.

6 Remove the risotto from the heat and and serve immediately.

Truly creamy & delicious, washed down with the remaining Prosecco!

Prosecco Turkey Meatballs

Ingredients

- **450g/1lb minced turkey**
- **½ onion, peeled and finely chopped**
- **1 rice cake, crumbled**
- **1 egg**
- **½ tsp salt**

- **Ground black pepper**
- **75g/3oz tomato puree**
- **200g/7oz cranberries, fresh or frozen**
- **½ tsp Dijon mustard**
- **250ml/1 cup Prosecco**

Method

1 Preheat the oven to 400F/200C/Gas6

2 Throw the turkey, onion and crumbled rice cake into a large bowl. Break in the egg and season with salt and pepper. Mix it all together with your hands. Shape it into 12 small meatballs and place each on a lined baking sheet.

3 Bake in the oven for 15-20 minutes or until cooked through.

4 Pour the tomato puree, cranberries, mustard and Prosecco into a large pan and cook on high heat until boiling.

5 Add the baked meatballs and stir to coat them thoroughly. Lower the heat and simmer, uncovered for 10 minutes.

6 Lovely served with pasta or rice.

Ideal as a festive starter or make fewer, larger meatballs for a main course.

Prosecco Oysters and Turbot

Ingredients

- **8 oysters, opened with juices retained**
- **1 shallot, peeled and shredded**
- **250ml/1 cup Prosecco**
- **2 tbsp double cream**
- **100g/3½oz butter**

- **Squeeze of lemon juice**
- **Salt & pepper**
- **4 turbot fillets, skinned**
- **1 large leek, finely shredded**
- **1 tbsp chervil, chopped**

Method

1 In a pan, gently warm the oysters in their juices for a couple of minutes. Remove from the heat.

2 In a different pan, heat the shallot with the Prosecco. Bring to the boil, and reduce the liquid by about half. Strain the oyster juice into the pan, and continuing to boil until the liquid reduces by another half. Pour in the cream and when it's simmering again, whisk in about three quarters of the butter, a little at a time. Add a squeeze of lemon juice, and season with salt and pepper. Set aside.

3 Divide the remaining butter between two frying pans and place both over medium heat. Once sizzling, place the turbot in one pan and the shredded leek in the other. Season both with salt and freshly ground black pepper. Fry until the turbot becomes light golden, then turn it. Cook the leek until softened.

4 Re-warm the sauce, and add the oysters and chervil. Divide the leeks between four bowls, and arrange the turbot and oysters on top. Spoon the Prosecco sauce over everything.

5 Serve immediately.

Enjoy this luxurious main course with a glass of chilled Prosecco.

Prosecco Salad Dressings

Ingredients

Option 1

- **2 tbsp extra virgin olive oil**
- **2 tbsp Prosecco**
- **½ tsp Dijon mustard**
- **1 tsp sugar**
- **¼ tsp garlic powder**
- **¼ tsp Italian seasoning**

Option 2

- **1 tsp wholegrain mustard**
- **1/4 teaspoon garlic powder**
- **1/4 teaspoon onion powder**
- **1 tbsp balsamic vinegar**
- **2 tsp maple syrup**
- **2 tbsp Prosecco**
- **2 tbsp extra virgin olive oil**

Method

1 For either option mix all the ingredients together in a small bowl or use a sterilised jam jar and vigoursly shake with the lid tightly fastened to blend the ingredients.

2 Add sea salt and black pepper to both dressings to really bring out the subtle flavours.

3 Drizzle over your favourite salad just before serving.

Guaranteed to add that extra special quality to even the simplest salad.

Prosecco Crepes

Ingredients

- **3 eggs**
- **250ml/1 cup milk**
- **250ml/1 cup Prosecco**
- **175g/6oz plain flour**

- **1 pinch salt**
- **2 tbsp combined olive oil and melted butter, plus more for frying**

Method

1 In a large bowl, whisk together the eggs, milk and Prosecco.

2 Add the flour and whisk again.

3 Add the salt and the oil and butter mixture and whisk again.

4 Chill the batter in the fridge for at least an hour or more.

5 Heat a non-stick frying pan over medium heat. Brush it with some oil and butter mixture. When the pan is hot but not smoking, pour in a little batter to make a thin crepe.

6 Cook for about a minute on the first side and 30 seconds on the other, until the crepe is golden brown.

7 Continue with the rest of batter. Fill the crepes with your favourite savoury (or sweet) toppings.

The Prosecco makes a beautifully light batter for thin crepes.

Prosecco Poached Salmon

Ingredients

- 1 bottle Prosecco
- 60ml/¼ cup white wine vinegar
- 1 bay leaf
- 1½ tsp salt
- 2 large salmon fillets

Method

1 Pour the Prosecco and vinegar into a large pan. Add the bay leaf,and salt and bring to the boil.

2 Reduce the heat. Place the salmon fillets in the pan and simmer for 10 minutes or until the salmon is cooked through and flakes easily with a fork.

3 Remove and serve with a large bowl of your favourite salad and fresh, crusty bread

Prosecco adds sparkle and romance to your salmon dish!

Prosecco Mussels

Serves 4

Ingredients

- 1 tbsp olive oil
- 1 tbsp crushed garlic
- 1 tbsp fresh mixed herbs

- Salt & pepper
- 900g/2lbs fresh mussels, cleaned
- 500ml/2 cups Prosecco

Method

1 Heat the oil in a large pan and sauté the garlic. Throw in the herbs, season with salt and pepper and cook for a couple minutes.

2 Turn up the heat and add the mussels and the Prosecco. Bring to the boil, cover and cook for about five minutes, or until the mussels are fully open.

3 Serve with some good, crusty bread.

Remember to throw away any mussels which don't open.

Prosecco Mushroom Sauce

Ingredients

- **250ml/1 cup vegetable stock**
- **15g/½oz porcini mushrooms**
- **500ml/2 cups Prosecco**
- **50g/2oz shallots, peeled and finely chopped**
- **50g/2oz unsalted butter, plus 40g/1½oz**
- **3 tbsp plain flour**
- **Salt & pepper**

Method

1 Pour the stock into a pan and add the porcini mushrooms. Cover and bring to the boil. Reduce the heat and leave to for a few minutes to allow the flavour to infuse.

2 In different pan,combine the Prosecco and the shallots. Bring to the boil and cook until the wine reduces by a little half. Remove from the heat then whisk in 50g butter.

3 In a third pan, heat the remaining 40g butter. When it's melted, stir in the flour and cook for about 5 minutes stirring frequently. Stirring constantly gradually pour in the mushrooms and stock.

4 Remove from the heat and whisk in the Prosecco & shallot mixture.

5 Strain into a bowl, to remove the mushrooms and shallots and leave you with a smooth sauce. Season to taste and keep warm, without boiling, until needed.

Delicious with turkey, pork or meaty fish.

Prosciutto & Prosecco Risotto

Ingredients

- **4 thin slices prosciutto ham**
- **750ml/3 cups chicken stock**
- **12 asparagus spears, cut into 1-inch pieces**
- **25g/1oz butter, divided**
- **1 shallot, peeled and finely chopped**
- **175g/6oz Arborio rice**
- **250ml/1 cup Prosecco**
- **25g/1oz freshly grated Parmesan cheese**
- **¼ tsp salt**
- **½ tsp freshly ground black pepper**

Method

1 Preheat the oven to 450F/230C/Gas7.

2 Bake the prosciutto slices for about 6 minutes, until crisp. Set aside for garnish.

3 In a saucepan bring the stock to the boil. Reduce the heat to a simmer. Drop in the asparagus and blanch it for 2 minutes before removing with a slotted spoon. Rinse the asparagus with cold water and set aside.

4 In another pan, melt half the butter. Add the shallot and cook for 3 minutes until tender. Add the rice and stir well.

5 Add the Prosecco and simmer until the liquid has almost evaporated. Keep adding the stock, a little at a time, stirring constantly, for about 20 minutes or until the rice is al dente.

6 Remove the pan from the heat. Gently stir in the asparagus, the remaining butter, Parmesan, salt, and pepper.

7 Serve the risotto garnished with the crispy prosciutto crumbled over the top. Serve immediately.

Prosecco Marinated Halibut

Ingredients

- 120ml/½ cup liquorice liqueur
- 2 tbsp honey
- 120ml/½ cup Prosecco
- Zest of ½ lemon
- 7g/¼oz mint leaves, chopped
- 1 chilli, de-seeded, cut in half lengthways
- 1 tbsp tarragon
- 4 halibut fillets
- Salt and pepper

Method

1 The day before you plan to eat this combine all the ingredients, except the fish and seasoning, into a large bowl.

2 Add the halibut and place in the fridge to marinate overnight.

3 When you're ready to cook, preheat the grill to Medium.

4 Remove the fish from the marinade and season it well with salt and pepper.

5 Slide the fish under the grill for 10-15 minutes until glazed and cooked.

Try this marinade with other fish too.

Tarragon Prosecco Chicken

Ingredients

- 1 tbsp olive oil
- 4 chicken breasts
- Salt & pepper, to taste
- 1 large shallot, peeled and finely chopped
- 250ml/1 cup Prosecco
- 15g/½oz unsalted butter
- 75g/3oz mushrooms, sliced
- 2 tbsp fresh tarragon
- Juice of 1 lemon juice

Method

1 Preheat the oven to 375F/190C/Gas5.

2 Heat the oil in a large frying pan. Add the chicken and seer for 3 minutes on each side. Remove the chicken to a plate and set aside.

3 Add the shallots to the pan and stir for a minute. Pour in the Prosecco, bring to the boil for just a moment. Lower the heat and scrape the bottom of the pan to loosen the cooked-on bits.

4 Place the chicken back in the pan and baste with the prosecco sauce. Transfer the pan to the oven and bake for 25 to 30 minutes or until the chicken is thoroughly cooked.

5 Meanwhile, heat the butter in a different pan. Throw in the mushrooms and sauté for 5 minutes.

6 Take the chicken out of the oven, and add the mushrooms. Stir in the tarragon and drizzle with lemon juice to taste.

Serve with rice or new potatoes and fresh green beans.

Scallops in Prosecco Sauce

Ingredients

- 1½ tbsp olive oil
- 675g/1½lb scallops
- 75g/3oz shiitake mushrooms, sliced
- 1 shallot, peeled and chopped
- 120ml/½ cup Prosecco
- 1 tbsp Dijon mustard
- ¼ tsp salt
- ¼ tsp dried tarragon
- 60ml/¼ cup soured cream

Method

1 Heat the oil in a large frying pan. Pat the scallops dry with kitchen towel, and place them in the pan. Cook them for 3 minutes on each side or until they're piping hot. Remove them from the pan and keep warm.

2 Add the mushrooms and shallots to the same pan. Fry them for about 3 minutes or until the liquid evaporates and the mushrooms darken. Stir in the Prosecco, mustard, salt, and tarragon. Scrape the pan with your spoon to loosen any cooked-on bits.

3 Remove the pan from the heat. Stir in the soured cream and pour over the scallops to serve.

The Prosecco and tarragon in this sauce make a perfect, delicate accompaniment to seafood.

Prosecco Salmon Tartare

Ingredients

- 120ml/½ cup pink Prosecco
- 400g/14oz fresh salmon, filleted, skinned, finely chopped
- Juice of 1 lime
- 1 avocado, peeled, finely diced
- 2 tsp fresh dill, chopped
- 1 shallot, peeled and finely chopped
- Salt & pepper
- 200g/7oz mayonnaise
- 1 tbsp tomato ketchup
- 2 tbsp brandy
- Dash Worcestershire sauce
- 12 king prawns, cooked, peeled
- 1 pink grapefruit, segmented

Method

1 Pour the Prosecco into a pan over medium heat. Bring to the boil and reduce the liquid by about a third.

2 In a bowl, mix together the salmon, lime juice, avocado, dill, shallot, and the reduced Prosecco. Season with salt and pepper.

3 In a separate bowl, stir together the mayonnaise, tomato ketchup, brandy and Worcestershire sauce.

4 Serve the salmon mixture onto 4 plates. Arrange three prawns and three segments of grapefruit on top of each, and drizzle with the mayonnaise dressing.

Neither the Prosecco nor the grapefruit have to be pink, but it does look prettier!

Prosecco Cheese Fondue

Ingredients

- ½ bottle Prosecco
- 1 shallot, finely chopped
- 500g/1lb2oz cream cheese, cut into 1-inch cubes
- 250g/9oz Gruyere cheese, grated
- 25g/1oz Parmesan cheese, grated
- 1 tbsp plain flour
- Pinch freshly grated nutmeg

Method

1 In a saucepan, heat the Prosecco with the shallot. Add the cream cheese and whisk until it has melted.

2 In a bowl, stir together the Gruyere, Parmesan and flour. Gradually whisk the mixture into the cream cheese mixture, a handful at a time as each batch of cheese melts.

3 When all the cheese is melted, bring the mixture to the boil, whisking continuously until the mixture is thick enough to coat the back of a spoon. Stir in the nutmeg.

4 Pour the mixture into a fondue pot and serve immediately.

Absolutely delicious served with chunky bread, crisp raw vegetables like broccoli and cauliflower and apple slices.

Festive Prosecco Ham

Ingredients

- **1.3kg/3lb gammon joint**
- **24 whole cloves**
- **Cooking spray**
- **250ml/1 cup Prosecco, plus 120ml/½ cup**
- **1 vanilla bean, split, seeds scraped out**
- **200g/7oz apple chutney**

Method

1 Preheat your oven to 350F/175C/Gas4 .

2 Trim the fat and rind from the ham. Score the outside in a diamond pattern, and press in an even scattering of cloves.

3 Spray a roasting tin with non-stick oil and place the gammon in it. Pour 250ml/1 cup of Prosecco over the ham. Bake in the oven for 30 mins.

4 Add the vanilla and the rest of the Prosecco to a small pan. Bring to the boil and cook for 2 minutes. Stir in the apple chutney and cook for 3 mins stirring constantly until the chutney dissolves.

5 Remove the pan from the heat. Pour half of this Prosecco sauce over the ham. Bake it for another half hour, then pour the rest of the Prosecco mixture over it and bake for another 30 minutes or until the ham is heated through. Rest the ham on a platter, covered loosely with foil for 15 minutes before serving.

Definitely a special occasion ham!

Seafood and Prosecco Pasta

Ingredients

- 2 tbsp olive oil
- 2 shallots, peeled and finely chopped
- 1 clove garlic, crushed
- 250ml/1 cup Prosecco
- 250ml/1 cup double cream
- Salt & pepper

- Handful fresh oregano, chopped
- Handful fresh basil, chopped
- 100g/3½oz butter
- 3 lobster tails, cut in half lengthwise
- 400g/14oz prawns
- 225g/8oz fresh pasta, e.g. linguine

Method

1 Heat the olive oil in a pan. Throw in half the shallots and half the garlic and cook gently until they are translucent. Add the Prosecco, bring to the boil and reduce the liquid by half.

2 Add the cream and season well with salt and pepper. Boil until the sauce thickens then stir in half the chopped basil and half the oregano.

3 In another pan, melt the butter until it foams. Throw in the remaining garlic and shallots then add the lobster tails, shell side down. Add the rest of the basil and oregano. When the lobster shells are bright red, turn them over and cook for another 5 minutes, or until the lobster meat is white and opaque. Remove them from the pan to a plate.

4 Add the prawns to the lobster pan and cook for about 4 minutes, until they are pink and cooked through. Remove them and set aside with the lobster.

5 Pour the buttery juices from the lobster and prawn pan into the cream sauce and whisk.

6 Boil the pasta in salted water until cooked. Drain and gently combine with the sauce, prawns and lobster tails to serve.

Prosecco Cheese Dip

Ingredients

- **450g/1lb assorted cheeses, cubed**
- **1 clove garlic, crushed**
- **250ml/1 cup Prosecco**
- **½ tbsp chopped fresh herbs**

Method

1 Throw all the ingredients into your food processor and blend until smooth.

2 Chill the dip in the fridge for at least one hour. Top with black pepper to taste.

3 Serve with crusty bread or crunchy vegetables.

Alternatively, spread the mixture on bread and grill for a luxurious version of cheese on toast.

Cucumber & Prosecco Salad

Ingredients

- 2 fresh cucumbers
- 3 spring onions
- 1 tbsp cider vinegar
- 1 tbsp caster sugar
- ½ lime

- Salt & pepper
- 100ml/3½ floz crème fraiche
- 50ml/2floz Prosecco
- 1 tbsp freshly chopped chives

Method

1 Cut the cucumbers into slices and cut each slice in half so they are half-moon shapes.

2 Finely slide the spring onions and add into a bowl along with the sliced cucumber.

3 Add in the cider vinegar and sugar, and squeeze in the juice of half a fresh lime. Mix well, tossing the cucumber and spring onions until evenly covered.

4 Add in a pinch of salt and pepper and toss the salad again. Drain any excess vinegar out of the bowl and place to one side.

5 Mix the crème fraiche and the prosecco until the two are blended well.

6 Mix in the freshly chopped Chives before adding the mixture to the cucumber salad. Gently combine the crème fraiche mixture in with the prepared cucumber and spring onion salad ready to serve.

Red Pesto & Bacon Prosecco Pasta

Ingredients

- 300g/11oz pasta
- Pinch of Salt
- 1 tbsp olive oil
- 200g/7oz bacon lardons

- 120ml/½ cup Prosecco
- 200g/7oz (or 1 jar) Red Pesto
- Grated Red Leicester cheese

Method

1 Boil the pasta in salted water 10–12 minutes. While the pasta is cooking heat the oil in a large frying pan.

2 Add the bacon lardons into the pan and fry for 2-3 minutes before adding the Prosecco.

3 Simmer for a further 3 to 4 minutes, or until the lardons are cooked through and the Prosecco reduces down to just a few teaspoons full.

4 Once cooked, drain the pasta and stir through the pesto. back in the pan. warm over a low heat until everything is piping hot.

5 Spoon into bowls and sprinkle on top the grated Red Leicester cheese to serve.

Truffle Prosecco Pasta

Ingredients

- 300g/11oz penne pasta
- Pinch of Salt
- 1 tbsp olive oil
- 200g/7oz chicken breast
- 120ml/ ½ cup Prosecco
- 75g/3oz truffle sauce
- Grated Parmesan cheese to serve

Method

1 Bring a large pan of water to boil. Add the pasta with a pinch of salt and boil for 10 – 12 minutes.

2 Meanwhile heat the oil in a large frying pan. Cut the chicken into slices and add them into the pan. Cook for 2 to 3 minutes, or until the chicken is sealed.

3 Add in the Prosecco and allow the chicken to simmer for another 4 to 5 minutes, or until the chicken is cooked through.

4 Once the chicken pieces are cooked, drain away the any excess oil and Prosecco and place to one side.

5 Drain the cooked pasta and stir through the cooked chicken and truffle sauce.

6 Warm well over a low heat until piping hot. Spoon into bowls and sprinkle over grated Parmesan cheese to serve.

This works just as well with spaghetti as a nice alternative.

Prosecco Chicken, Bacon & Pea One-Pot

Ingredients

- **4 rashers of bacon**
- **1 tbsp olive oil**
- **500g/1lb 2oz chicken breast**
- **250ml/1 cup Prosecco**
- **1 onion**
- **1 leek**

- **500ml/2 cups chicken stock**
- **1 garlic clove, crushed**
- **1tbsp wholegrain mustard**
- **1 tsp dried mixed herbs**
- **Salt & pepper**
- **100g/3½oz frozen peas**

Method

1 Grill the bacon until crispy, cut into small pieces and put to one side.

2 Put a casserole dish on a medium heat and heat the oil for a few minutes. Dice the chicken and add to the dish.

3 Seal the chicken and then before adding the Prosecco. Lower the heat slightly so that the chicken continues to simmer in the Prosecco. Dice the onion and slice the leeks and then add these to the casserole dish too.

4 Allow to simmer for 3-4 mins then add the chicken stock and garlic stirring well. Mix in mustard, herbs, salt and pepper to season.

5 Stir in the frozen peas and allow to simmer for another 2 to 3 minutes.

6 Combine everything well, cover and leave to simmer on a very low heat for 1½ to 2 hours before serving.

Serve with creamy mashed potato.

Chorizo, Prosecco & Feta Warm Side Salad

Ingredients

- 2 red onions
- 4 spring onions
- 1 tbsp olive oil
- 250g/9oz Chorizo
- 120ml/½ cup Prosecco

- 400g/14oz tinned chickpeas
- 1 clove of garlic, crushed
- ½ tsp paprika
- ½ tsp chilli powder
- 200g/7oz Feta cheese

Method

1 Finely cut the red onions & spring onions and place in the salad bowl.

2 Heat the oil in a frying pan. Finely cube the chorizo place in the pan and stir over a medium heat for 1 to 2 minutes. Add in the Prosecco and allow the chorizo to simmer for a further 2 to 3 minutes or until the chorizo is starting to brown.

3 Drain the chickpeas before adding to the pan along with the garlic.

4 Sprinkle in the paprika and chilli, stir and allow to simmer for a further 1-2 minutes on a low heat.

5 Remove from the heat and add the chorizo, spices and juices into the salad bowl and toss the mixture with the onion and spring onion.

6 Cut the Feta cheese into cubes and add on top of the salad ready to serve.

Serve warm to accompany chicken fillets or pork chops.

Strawberry, Prosecco & Mint Salsa

Ingredients

- 1 tbsp olive oil
- 500g/1lb strawberries
- 1½ tbsp strawberry liquor

- 120ml/½ cup Prosecco
- 1½ tbsp brown sugar
- A bunch of fresh mint leaves

Method

1 Heat the oil in a saucepan. Remove the stems from the strawberries and cut them into quarters.

2 Add the cut strawberries to the pan and cook over a medium heat for 2-3 minutes, stirring regularly to break the strawberries down.

3 Mix the strawberry liquor into the pan and simmer for another minute or so before adding the Prosecco and sugar. Combine the mixture well and allow to simmer on a low heat for another 4-5 minutes, stirring regularly.

4 Finely cut the mint leaves and add to the mixture. Mix well one last time and bring off the heat ready to serve.

Serve warm with a white meat main or allow to cool and serve with fish.

Garlic, Lemon and Prosecco Prawns

Ingredients

- 1 tbsp olive oil
- 500g/1lb2oz uncooked prawns
- 3 cloves of garlic, crushed
- 120ml/ ½ cup Prosecco

- ½ lemon
- Salt & pepper
- Small bunch of parsley

Method

1 Heat the olive oil on a medium heat while you wash and drain the prawns. Place the prawns in the pan and allow them to cook and begin to turn pink. Add the garlic to the prawns and cook for 1 to 2 minutes.

2 Add the Prosecco to the pan and simmer on a low heat until cooked through.

3 Squeeze the juice of half a fresh lemon into the pan and season with salt and pepper.

4 Finely chop the fresh parsley and stir in with the garlic and Prosecco prawn mixture.

5 Serve straight from the pan while they are hot; you can serve along with the pan juices or drain first depending on your preferences. This can make a great addition to a meal or work as a tapas dish alongside others.

Serve with a mayonnaise or crème fraiche dip.

Creamy Mushroom and Prosecco Chicken

Serves 4

Ingredients

- 1 tbsp olive oil
- 500g/1lb 2oz chicken breasts
- 1 onion, diced
- 200g/7oz mushrooms, diced
- 250ml/1 cup Prosecco
- 1 clove of garlic, crushed
- 250ml/1 cup crème fraiche
- Salt & pepper

Method

1 Heat the olive oil in the pan on a medium heat whilst cutting the chicken breasts into slices. Add the sliced chicken to the pan along the onion, garlic and mushrooms. Cook for 2-3 minutes.

2 Add the Prosecco to the pan and allow the chicken, mushrooms and onion to simmer for a further 2-3 minutes. Simmer until the onion and mushrooms begin to soften, the chicken is cooked through and some of the Prosecco has evaporated off.

3 Bring the pan to a lower heat and gently mix in the crème fraiche, adding salt and pepper to season.

4 Allow the mixture to heat through, but ensure that it does not boil or bubble too much. Take off the heat and serve straight away.

Serve with rice or potatoes and seasonal vegetables.

Prosecco & Mustard Pork

Ingredients

- 2 tbsp olive oil
- 1 clove of garlic
- 1 tbsp French mustard

- 4 large pork chops
- 120ml/ ½ cup Prosecco
- Salt & pepper

Method

1 Heat the olive oil in a large pan on a medium heat. Crush the garlic and mix with the mustard.

2 Place the pork chops in the pan and lightly smooth across half of the mustard paste.

3 Add the Prosecco to the pan and cook for 5 to 6 minutes or until the pork chop begins to seal.

4 Turn the pork chops over and smooth the remaining mustard paste across the pork chop.

5 Season with salt and pepper and cook for another 5 to 6 minutes in the Prosecco or until the pork chops are cooked through. Ensure the meat is piping hot before serving.

Serve with Lyonnaise potatoes and green beans.

Super Simple Prosecco Chicken & Tomato

Ingredients

- 1 tbsp olive oil
- 500g/1lb2oz chicken breasts
- 200g/7oz cherry tomatoes
- 120ml/½ cup Prosecco
- 1 clove of garlic, crushed
- 2 tins of chicken soup
- Salt & pepper

Method

1 Preheat the oven to 350F/180C/Gas4.

2 Cut the chicken breasts into slices and finely dice the tomatoes. Heat the olive oil in a pan on a medium heat and add the chicken and tomatoes to the pan.

3 Once the chicken is sealed, add in the Prosecco & garlic and simmer for 3-4 mins.

4 Add the contents of the pan, including juices, into a casserole dish. Pour the chicken soup into the dish and combine well.

5 Cover and place in the oven for 45 minutes; you can cook on a lower heat for 1 to 2 hours – perfect for preparing in the early evening ready to eat later fuss-free!

Serve with new potatoes or creamy mashed potatoes.

Prosecco Yorkshire Puddings

Ingredients

- Small jug of olive oil
- 300g/10oz plain flour
- 4 eggs

- 150ml/5floz milk
- 50ml/2floz Prosecco
- Salt & pepper

Method

1 Pre-heat oven to 190'C/375F/Gas5. Drizzle a small amount of olive oil into each cup of the pudding tray Add enough to thinly cover the bottom of each section but not too much to 'drown' the mixture when added. Place in the oven when heated and leave for 10 minutes.

2 Sieve the flour into a bowl. Crack the eggs and whisk into the flour until a thick batter is created. Pour a small amount of the milk into the mixture and fold it in until a smoother batter is formed. Gradually add more of the milk, as well as the Prosecco, and repeat this process until a light batter

is created with a consistency similar to double cream.

3 Remove the tray and hot oil from the oven and pour the batter mixture into each section approximately 1cm deep. Place in the oven and cook for 20 – 30 minutes.

Whilst cooking, do not open the oven door; this will prevent the Yorkshires from rising properly.

Peppercorn & Prosecco Sauce

Ingredients

- **50g/2oz butter**
- **1 shallot**
- **75ml/3floz beef stock**
- **3 tbsp black peppercorns**

- **75ml/3floz Prosecco**
- **75ml/3floz brandy**
- **75ml/3floz double cream**

Method

1 Heat the butter in the pan on a medium heat. Finely dice the shallot and add to the pan. Cook for 2 to 3 minutes or until the shallot begins to soften.

2 Add the beef stock in the pan and allow it to simmer whilst you crush the peppercorns in a mortar to a coarse powder.

3 Add the crushed peppercorns to the pan and allow to simmer for 2 to 3 minutes. Add in the Prosecco and Brandy, stirring well, and allow the mixture to simmer for a further 2 to 3 minutes.

4 Just before removing from the heat to serve, stir in the double cream, warming through but being careful not to boil the now creamy mixture and serve immediately.

Serve with a perfectly cooked steak and chips.

Prosecco & Chive Prawns

Ingredients

- **3 onions, chopped**
- **75g/3oz butter**
- **450g/9oz king prawns**
- **3 tbsp cognac**
- **250ml/1 cup Prosecco**
- **120ml/½ cup double cream cream**
- **2 tbsp freshly chopped chives**
- **Salt and pepper**

Method

1 Heat the butter in a saucepan and sauté the onions for a few minutes until softened and golden.

2 Add the prawns and cook for a few minutes. Stir in the the cognac and Prosecco and cook for a further 5 minutes or until the prawns are pink and piping hot.

3 Pour in the cream and gently warm through.

4 Season well and garnish with chives to serve.

Delicate, light & creamy

Prosecco Sweet Recipes

Prosecco Truffles

Ingredients

For the filling:
- **150ml/5floz double cream**
- **25g/1oz unsalted butter**
- **100g/3½oz dark chocolate, finely chopped**
- **60ml/¼ cup Prosecco**

- **50g/2oz milk chocolate, finely chopped**

For the coating:
- **150g/5oz milk chocolate**
- **Icing sugar**

Method

1 Heat the cream and butter in a pan until the butter has melted and starts to simmer. Throw the chopped chocolate into a large, heatproof bowl. Pour the hot cream and butter mixture over the chocolate. Leave for a couple of minutes, then stir until all the chocolate has melted completely.

2 Stir in the Prosecco. Chill the mixture for at least 4 hours in the fridge, or overnight.

3 Line 2 baking trays with foil. Pipe the mixture, shaping into 25 small balls on the trays. Slide the trays into the freezer for at least an hour or until you're nearly ready to serve them.

4 For the coating, throw the milk chocolate into another heatproof bowl. Heat it in the microwave until melted, stirring after every half-minute or so.

5 Drop a frozen truffle into the melted chocolate and turn it with a spoon to coat it. Place back onto the foil lined tray and repeat to coat all the truffles. Leave them to set for about 10 minutes.

6 Once set, dust the truffles with icing sugar. Serve and enjoy.

Prosecco Pancakes

Serves 2

Ingredients

For the pancakes:
- **225g/8oz plain flour**
- **2 tsp baking powder**
- **1 tsp bicarbonate of soda**
- **250ml/1 cup buttermilk**
- **4 tbsp Prosecco**

- **2 eggs**
- **Clotted cream and berries**

For the syrup:
- **150g/5oz sugar**
- **120ml/½ cup Prosecco**

Method

1 To make the pancakes, mix together in a bowl the plain flour, baking powder and bicarbonate of soda. Make a well in the middle of the mixture and pour in the buttermilk and the Prosecco. Break in the eggs and then beat the mixture until smooth.

2 Allow the batter to rest for an hour.

3 Then heat a buttered pan and pour in a small scoop of the batter. Cook on both sides. Repeat until you've used all the batter.

4 To make the syrup, simply heat the sugar and the Prosecco in a pan for around 3 minutes, until it becomes syrupy.

5 Pile the pancakes on a plate, and top them with clotted cream and berries. Then pour the syrup over the top.

6 Serve and enjoy!

A special grown up treat for Pancake Day! Enjoy with raspberries, strawberries, blueberries or cherries.

Prosecco & Strawberry Jellies

Ingredients

- **120ml/½ cup water**
- **200g/7oz caster sugar**
- **6 sheets leaf gelatine**
- **1 bottle Prosecco**

- **450g/1lb strawberries, hulled and halved, plus 12 more, quartered, for decoration**

Method

1 Heat the water and sugar in a pan until the sugar has completely dissolved. Add the strawberries, bring to the boil, and simmer for about 5 minutes or until the strawberries are soft and the liquid is red and syrupy.

2 Strain the syrup into a large jug, without pushing the strawberries through the sieve. Allow to cool. Discard the cooked strawberries.

3 Meanwhile, soak the gelatine in a bowl of cold water. When it's soft, squeeze the excess water from the gelatine sheets and stir them into the syrup until completely melted.

4 Divide the decoration strawberries between 6 Champagne flutes.

5 Mix the Prosecco into the strawberry syrup, then pour the mixture into the glasses.

6 Chill overnight, and serve.

Make also with other fruits, e.g. clementines, raspberries etc.

Pink Prosecco Buttercream

Serves 6

Ingredients

- **2 egg whites**
- **140g/4½oz sugar**
- **1 tbsp pink edible glitter**

- **120ml/½ cup pink Prosecco**
- **225g/8oz butter, softened at room temperature**

Method

1 In a bowl, hand-whisk the egg whites until foamy. Stir in the sugar, and Prosecco. Place the bowl over a pan of boiling water and continue whisking until the sugar has dissolves and the mixture is piping hot.

2 Remove the bowl from the heat and use an electric mixer on high speed to whisk until it cools.

3 Gradually add the butter, a little at a time, mixing well between each addition and stir in the glitter.

4 Use a spatula or piping bag to add your buttercream to your favourite cakes.

Ideal for meringues, macaroons, cupcakes etc.

Strawberry Prosecco Cupcakes

Serves 6

Ingredients

- *For the sponge:*
- **1 box strawberry cake mix**
- **75ml/2½floz vegetable oil**
- **3 egg whites**
- **250ml/1 cup Prosecco**
- **140g/4½oz strawberries, diced**

For the frosting:
- **375g/13oz icing sugar**
- **75g/3oz butter, softened**
- **1½ tsp vanilla extract**
- **3 tbsp Prosecco**

For the topping:
- **4 strawberries, sliced**
- **1 tsp sugar**

Method

1 Preheat the oven according to the cake mix instructions. Grease a cupcake tin.

2 To make the cupcakes, beat the cake mix together with the oil, egg whites and Prosecco, until combined and bubbly. Fold in the diced strawberries, then spoon the mixture into the cupcake tin until each cup is about two-thirds full.

3 Bake in the oven for around 20 minutes or until the cakes are cooked through. Set aside to cool.

4 To make the frosting, beat the sugar and butter together in a bowl. Gradually stir in the vanilla and Prosecco, until the mixture is smooth and spreadable. Spread it across the top of each cupcake.

5 To make the strawberry topping, sprinkle sugar over the strawberry slices and leave them for 20 minutes to release their juices. Add a strawberry slice to the top of each cupcake.

6 Enjoy!

Chocolate Prosecco Frosting

Ingredients

- 250ml/1 cup Prosecco, plus 2 tbsp
- 175g/6oz dark chocolate
- 225g/8oz unsalted butter, softened
- 375g/13oz icing sugar

Method

1 In a small pan, heat the cup of Prosecco. Bring to the boil, reduce the heat and simmer for about 15 minutes to reduce. Remove it from the heat and leave to cool.

2 Melt the chocolate in the microwave.

3 In a food processor, beat the softened butter until fluffy. Whisk in the melted chocolate, and the reduced Prosecco. Add the other 2 tablespoons of Prosecco and whisk again until smooth.

4 Gradually whisk in the icing sugar until the mixture is light and fluffy.

5 Swirl onto your favourite cakes or desserts.

This decadent frosting is deal for spreading on cupcakes, sponges and biscuits, but too soft for intricate piping work.

Prosecco Custard

Ingredients

- **6 egg yolks**
- **125g/4oz caster sugar**
- **250ml/1 cup milk**

- **120ml/½ cup single cream**
- **60ml/¼ cup Prosecco**
- **1 vanilla pod, split, seeds scraped out**

Method

1 Whisk the egg yolks and sugar together in a bowl until fluffy.

2 In a pan, heat the milk, cream, Prosecco and vanilla seeds until simmering. Remove the pan from the heat and gradually pour the liquid over the egg and sugar mixture, whisking continuously.

3 Pour the custard into to a clean pan and heat gently for about 10 minutes, stirring continuously, until the mixture is thick enough to coat the back of a spoon.

4 Serve with your favourite dessert.

Delicious alone or with fruit tarts and sponges.

Prosecco Lavender & Lemon Cake

Ingredients

For the sponge:
- **2 boxes lemon cake mix**
- **6 eggs**
- **600ml/1pt Prosecco, plus 60ml/¼ cup**

For the frosting:
- **350g/12oz butter, softened**
- **1.35kg/3lb icing sugar**
- **3 tsp lavender extract**
- **Juice from 3 lemons**
- **Sprinkles**

Method

1 Preheat the oven according to the cake intsructions. Grease and flour 4 cake tins.

2 Empty the cake mixes into a large bowl. Break in the eggs and pour in 600ml of the Prosecco (don't worry if it bubbles up). Mix on medium speed for 1-2 minutes or until the batter is smooth.

3 Divide the mix between the cake tins and bake in the oven according to package directions.

4 Meanwhile, to make the frosting, whisk the butter until smooth and creamy. Add in the icing sugar, lemon juice, lavender extract and the remaining 60ml Prosecco. Whisk until the mixture is smooth.

5 Spread frosting onto the first cake, then layer the cakes with frosting between and over the top of the final cake.

6 Chill in the fridge for half an hour.

7 Cover the top edge and the sides with sprinkles.

If you wish, add purple food colouring to the frosting.

White Chocolate Prosecco Fondue

Ingredients

- 100g/3½oz white chocolate chips
- 3 squares white cooking chocolate
- 120ml/½ cup double cream
- 3 tbsp Prosecco

Method

1 In a pan, heat the chocolate chips, chocolate squares, and cream over a low heat until smooth.

2 Stir in the Prosecco.

3 Transfer to a fondue pot and keep warm.

Serve with fingers of cake, fruit and biscuits for dipping.

Prosecco Peaches and Yogurt

Ingredients

- 1 bottle Prosecco
- 225g/8oz sugar
- 1 tbsp peach liqueur
- 1 tsp lemon juice
- Pinch salt

- 4 large peaches, peeled, stoned, quartered
- 500g/1lb2oz coconut flavoured yogurt
- Fresh basil leaves, to garnish

Method

1 Pour the Prosecco into a large pan. Stir in the sugar, liqueur, lemon juice and sea salt. Bring to a simmer. Add the peach slices and simmer for about 15 minutes, until the peaches are just tender.

2 Remove the pan from the heat and leave to cool. Then refrigerate for at least 4 hours, preferably overnight.

3 When you're ready to eat, dish the yogurt into bowls. Top with the chilled peaches in their syrup, and serve garnished with basil leaves.

Un-ripened peaches work best with this recipe.

Prosecco Raspberry Sorbet

Ingredients

- **4 scoops raspberry sorbet**
- **250ml/1 cup Prosecco**
- **2 slices plain sponge, cubed**
- **1 tsp sugar**
- **Whipped cream**

Method

1 Place the cake cubes in a frying pan, and sprinkle them with the sugar. Cook over gentle heat, stirring occasionally, until the edges are golden brown and the sugar begins to smell caramelized. Remove from heat and leave to cool.

2 Drop 2 scoops of sorbet into each serving dish. Pour the Prosecco over the top, then divide the sponge cubes between the dishes. Add a dollop of whipped cream and serve at once.

This is delicious with any fruit sorbet, e.g. orange, blackcurrant etc.

Prosecco Grape Granita

Ingredients

- 300g/11oz green seedless grapes, plus 4 to garnish.
- 120ml/½ cup Prosecco
- 2 tbsp sugar
- 2 tbsp lemon juice

Method

1 Blend the grapes into a puree, then strain the puree into a dish, pushing it through a sieve with the back of a spoon. Discard the skins.

2 Pour in the Prosecco, sugar, and lemon juice, and stir until the sugar dissolves.

3 Cover the dish and freeze for 4 hours. Give it a stir every hour.

4 When you're ready to eat it, fluff the mixture with a fork. Scoop into serving bowls and garnish with the remaining grapes.

5 Serve and enjoy!

A light, refreshing yet decadent dessert!

Raspberry Prosecco Sauce

Ingredients

- **120ml/½ cup Prosecco**
- **175g/6oz caster sugar**
- **200g/7oz fresh raspberries**

Method

1 Heat the Prosecco and sugar in a pan and bring to the boil. Lower the heat and simmer for 10 minutes.

2 Remove the pan from the heat, then gently stir in the raspberries. Set the mixture aside to cool.

3 When cool, blend the sauce until smooth, and pass it through a sieve to get rid of the seeds.

4 Serve with your favourite dessert.

This sauce will add a touch of delicious luxury to an ordinary fruit tart or ice cream.

Frozen Orange Mimosa

Ingredients

- **1 bottle Prosecco**
- **600ml/1pt orange juice**
- **175g/6oz honey**

Method

1 Mix the Prosecco with the orange juice and honey, stirring until thoroughly combined.

2 Pour the mixture into a freezer-proof container and freeze for about 4 hours, stirring it every hour or so. If possible, then leave it to freeze solid overnight.

3 Serve as a dessert or drink!

This is best with freshly squeezed orange juice – you'll need 9 or 10 oranges. And if you have an ice cream maker, you can follow its instructions rather than using the freezer.

White Prosecco Cake Balls

Ingredients

For the chocolate coating:
- **1 box strawberry cake mix**
- **½ bottle Prosecco**
- **4 tbsp vegetable oil**
- **3 eggs**
- **450g/1lb white cake frosting**

For the chocolate coating:
- **675g/1½lb white chocolate chips or cooking chocolate**
- **2 tbsp vegetable oil**

Method

1 Preheat the oven according to the cake intsructions. Line a 9x13-inch baking tin and set aside.

2 In a large bowl, whisk together the cake mix, Prosecco, eggs and 4 tablespoons of oil. Pour into the baking tin. Bake in the oven for about 30 minutes, or until the cake is cooked through. Remove it from oven and leave to cool

3 When cool, chop the cake roughly and crumble into a mixer or food processor. Add the frosting and whisk until thoroughly combined. Cover the bowl and chill in the fridge for at least 2 hours.

4 Line a fresh baking tray. Roll about a tablespoon of the cake mixture in your hands to form a ball. Place the ball on the baking tray and repeat until all the mixture is used. Refrigerate for another couple of hours.

5 Melt the white chocolate in the microwave until smooth. Stir in the vegetable oil.

6 Drop the cake balls into the melted chocolate to coat each thoroughly, and replace them on the baking tray to set. Once the shells are hard, serve and enjoy!

Prosecco and Orange Crème Brulee

Ingredients

- 2 tbsp Prosecco
- 125g/4oz orange segments, plus 6 thin orange slices, peeled
- 500ml/2 cups double cream
- 1 tbsp orange zest
- 1 vanilla bean, slit, seeds scraped out
- 8 egg yolks
- 5 tbsp sugar, plus ½ tsp
- 6 tbsp caster sugar

Method

1 Throw the orange segments into a bowl. Sprinkle half a teaspoon of sugar over the top and pour in the Prosecco.

2 In a pan, mix the cream and orange zest and add the vanilla seeds. In a bowl, whisk together the eggs and 5 tablespoons of sugar until thick.

3 Heat the pan of orange cream until just beginning to simmer. Remove from the heat and ladle into the egg mixture, whisking immediately. Then pour the egg mixture into the orange cream in the pan.

4 Turn the heat back on to low and cook, whisking constantly, until the mixture is thick enough to coat the back of a spoon. Set aside.

5 Use a slotted spoon to divide the marinated orange segments between each serving bowl (ideally ramekins). From the juice left behind in the bowl, add 1½ tablespoons of it to the custard, and stir it in.

6 Pour the custard over the orange segments. Then, gently press one thin orange slice on top. Refrigerate for at least 4 hours, or overnight.

7 When you're ready to serve, sprinkle each creme brulee with caster sugar. Pop under the grill for a few moments to brown.

Prosecco & Strawberry Compote

Ingredients

- 1kg/2¼lb strawberries, hulled
- 1kg/2¼lb sugar
- ½ tsp lemon juice
- 25g/1oz butter
- 120ml/½ cup Prosecco

Method

1 In a large pan, gently heat together the strawberries, sugar and lemon juice. When the sugar has all dissolved, turn up the heat and boil rapidly for 5 minutes.

2 Remove the pan from the heat and stir in the butter. Allow to cool for 15 minutes, then stir in the Prosecco.

3 Pour into sterilised jars.

Spread on freshly made scones and top with clotted cream for an extra special cream tea.

Prosecco Poached Strawberries

Ingredients

- 250ml/1 cup Prosecco
- 50g/2oz caster sugar
- 1 vanilla bean, seeds removed
- 250g/8oz strawberries hulled and halved

Method

1 In a pan heat together the Prosecco and caster sugar, stirring to dissolve the sugar.

2 Add the vanilla seeds. Bring to the boil then lower the heat and simmer until the liquid reduces by about half.

3 Meanwhile place the strawberry halves in a large bowl. When the Prosecco syrup has reduced, pour it over the strawberries, cover and chill in the fridge until ready to serve.

Delicious on its own, with ice cream, or with meringue nests and whipped cream.

Prosecco Biscuits

Ingredients

- **500ml/2 cups pink Prosecco**
- **125g/4oz plain flour**
- **1 tsp baking powder**

- **225g/8oz sugar, divided**
- **75g/3oz vegetable fat**

Method

1 Heat the Prosecco in a pan over high heat. Bring to the boil for about 15 minutes, until the liquid reduces by more than half. Set aside to cool thoroughly.

2 Mix the flour and baking powder in a large bowl.

3 In a different bowl cream half the sugar with the vegetable fat until smooth. Stir in the cooled Prosecco. Add the flour mixture and combine to a soft dough.

4 Heat the oven to 375F/190C/Gas5. Line two baking trays with parchment paper. Shape the dough into 1-inch balls, rolling each in the remaining sugar before placing on the baking tray. Using your fingers dipped in sugar, lightly press down the dough into biscuit shapes. Bake the biscuits in the oven for 10-15 minutes until golden.

5 Transfer to a cooling rack and cool. Serve as they are or spread with icing.

These make a delicious, sweet snack on their own, or as part of a dessert.

Pink Prosecco Cake

Ingredients

- **250g/9oz self-raising flour**
- **1¼ tsp baking powder**
- **¼ tsp baking soda**
- **¾ tsp salt**
- **500g/1lb2oz sugar**
- **140g/4½oz butter**
- **250ml/1 cup Prosecco**

- **3 tbsp vegetable oil**
- **2 tsp vanilla extract**
- **6 egg yolks**
- **3 egg whites**
- **½ tsp pink natural food colouring**
- **Raspberry jam**

For the buttercream:
- **125g/4oz butter**
- **125g/4oz vegetable fat**
- **450g/1lb icing sugar**
- **½ tsp vanilla extract**
- **¼ tsp salt**
- **60ml/¼ cup pink Prosecco**

Method

1 Preheat the oven to 350F/180C/Gas4. Grease three 8-inch cake tins and line them with parchment paper.

2 Mix together the flour, baking powder, baking soda, salt and 1lb of the sugar. In a different bowl, whisk together the butter, Prosecco, oil, vanilla and egg yolks.

3 Using a mixer, whisk the egg whites on medium speed until they're foamy. Slowly add the other 2oz sugar and continue whisking until the egg whites form stiff peaks. Transfer to another bowl.

4 Reusing your mixer, beat the flour mix with the butter and Prosecco mix until smooth. Stir in the food colouring. Gently

fold in the egg whites, then pour the batter in to the cake tins. Bake in the oven for 35 minutes then allow to cool.

5 Meanwhile, make the buttercream. Cream together the butter and vegetable fat, then gradually add the icing sugar. Once they are thoroughly combined, add the vanilla, salt and Prosecco. Mix until the buttercream is smooth and fluffy.

6 Once the cakes are cool, spread raspberry jam on the first cake, place the next layer on top of the jam, and spread on more jam. Add the third cake and spread the buttercream on the top and all around the whole, layered cake.

Prosecco Orange Chocolate Truffles

Ingredients

- **200g/7oz dark chocolate, chopped**
- **60ml/¼ cup double cream**
- **3 tbsp Prosecco**
- **1 tsp grated orange zest**
- **Cacao powder for coating**

Method

1 Gently melt the dark chocolate together with cream in in the microwave. Stir occasionally.

2 Combine in the Prosecco and orange zest.

3 Allow to cool for a few hours, or overnight in the fridge.

4 Using a melon scoop, scoop small balls from the chilled chocolate and cream mixture. Roll each ball in cacao powder.

5 Serve and enjoy!

These will keep well in an air-tight container in the fridge for up to a week.

Orange Blossom and Prosecco Buttercream

Ingredients

- ½ bottle Prosecco
- 350g/12oz unsalted butter
- 500g/1lb2oz icing sugar
- ¼ tsp orange blossom water

Method

1 In a pan gently heat the Prosecco until it reduces to about 1 tablespoon. Allow it to cool.

2 Once cold, pour it into your food mixer and throw in all the other ingredients. Whisk on low speed until the icing sugar is thoroughly combined, then increase to medium until the buttercream reaches the consistency you want.

3 Spread on your favourite cakes, biscuits and macaroons.

This subtly delicious buttercream will keep in the fridge for a week, or in the freezer for up to 3 months. So use as much or as little as you like at a time!

Prosecco Parfait

Ingredients

For the berries:
- **200g/7oz mixed berries, e.g. blueberries, raspberries, blackberries**
- **120ml/½ cup Prosecco**

For the cake:
- **1 box vanilla cake mix**
- **370ml/1½ cups Prosecco**
- **1 tsp vanilla extract**
- **Zest of 1 orange**

For the syrup:
- **50g/2oz butter, melted**
- **2 tbsp water**
- **125g/4oz sugar**
- **60ml/¼ cup Prosecco**
- **1 tbsp orange juice**
- **250ml/1 cup double cream, whipped, to serve**

Method

1 Soak the berries in Prosecco for about half an hour, then drain the berries when you're ready to serve.

2 Preheat the oven to 350°F/180C/Gas4.

3 In a bowl, stir together the cake mix, Prosecco, vanilla extract and orange zest. Pour it into a cake tin and bake for around 20 minutes or until cooked through. Allow to cool.

4 For the syrup, melt the butter in a pan. Whisk in the water and sugar. Bring to the boil, stirring occasionally, to thicken. Remove it from the heat and stir in the Prosecco and orange juice.

5 Slice up the cake and drop a piece in the bottom of each of 6 large glasses or serving dishes. Add a spoonful of the marinated berries, then drizzle over some of the Prosecco syrup. Add another layer of cake, then berries and syrup. Top with whipped cream.

6 Serve and enjoy!

Deliciously decadent and fun to enjoy with friends.

Prosecco Mousse

Ingredients

- **250ml/1 cup double cream**
- **4 egg yolks**
- **50g/2oz sugar, plus 2 tbsp**
- **½ bottle Prosecco, plus 3 tbsp**
- **2½ tsp powdered gelatine**

Method

1 Whip the cream into stiff peaks and set aside in the fridge.

2 Place a saucepan filled 1/3 with water over medium-high heat until water is simmering.

3 Whisk the egg yolks and sugar in a heatproof bowl. Pour in the Prosecco and whisk again.

4 Place the bowl over a pan of simmering water and whisk constantly as the mixture thickens. When it's nice and thick and lost its foaminess, remove the bowl from the heat and whisk for another minute. Set aside.

5 Place 3 tbsp Prosecco in a small microwave-safe bowl. Sprinkle on the gelatine powder and leave it for about 5 minutes until it's absorbed. Then heat the bowl in the microwave for about 10 seconds, or until the gelatine has melted completely.

6 Whisk the gelatine into the Prosecco mixture. Gently fold in the whipped cream. Spoon or pipe into 8 glasses and put them in the fridge until you're ready to serve.

Prosecco and Lemon Syllabub

Ingredients

- **8 ginger biscuits**
- **120ml/½ cup Prosecco**
- **250ml/1 cup double cream**
- **4 tbsp icing sugar**

- **8 tbsp lemon curd**
- **2 tbsp flaked almonds, toasted, to serve**
- **Fresh strawberries, to serve**

Method

1 Crumble the biscuits into the bottom of a transparent serving dish and moisten with half of the Prosecco.

2 Whip the cream with the sugar until it forms soft peaks then fold in the rest of the Prosecco.

3 Swirl the lemon curd through the cream to create a yellow marbling.

4 Spoon the mixture over the biscuit crumbs in the dish, and scatter with the toasted almonds and strawberries.

Feel free to substitute raspberries or other fruit for the strawberries.

Almond & Prosecco Poached Pears

Ingredients

- 1 bottle Prosecco
- 250ml/1 cup water
- 275g/10oz sugar, divided
- 1 vanilla bean, slit, seeds scraped out
- 4 whole pears, peeled and cored
- ½ tsp pure almond extract

Method

1 In a pan, combine the Prosecco, water, and 200g of the sugar. Whisk in the vanilla seeds. Bring to the boil, stirring occasionally.

2 Place the pears in the pan and turn down the heat to simmer. Place a smaller pan lid over the pears to keep them submerged.

3 Simmer for half an hour, turning the pears every few minutes until they are tender.

4 Using a slotted spoon, remove the pears and place them in separate bowls or glasses.

5 Strain the remaining liquids from the pan and return them. Stir in the remaining 75g/3oz sugar. Bring to the boil and cook until the liquid has reduced to about 1/3 of the original amount.

6 Remove from the heat and stir in the almond extract. Pour the syrup over the pears and serve.

Perfect with whipped cream or vanilla ice cream.

Prosecco-Soaked Berries Cream

Ingredients

- **200g/7oz strawberries**
- **150g/5oz raspberries**
- **250ml/1 cup Prosecco**
- **Fresh cream to serve**

Method

1 Remove the stalks and leaves from the strawberries and cut into halves or quarters, depending on the size of the strawberry.

2 Place the cut strawberries and whole raspberries in a bowl and pour over the Prosecco. Cover the bowl and leave the berries to soak in Prosecco for at least one hour, stirring the berries after half an hour to ensure an even soak. You can either store in the fridge or just to one side.

3 When you are ready to serve drizzle fresh cream over the top. Also good whipped.

4 Why not prepare these the day before to make life easier? The berries can be left in soak and stored in the fridge overnight which adds even more flavour.

Serve with dark chocolate shavings too.

Quick and Simple Prosecco Biscuits

Ingredients

- **100g/3½ oz butter**
- **50g/2oz caster sugar**
- **175g/6oz plain flour**

- **1 tsp Prosecco**
- **1 tsp vanilla extract**

Method

1 Pre-heat the oven to 160'C/325F/Gas3. Cover a baking tray with greaseproof paper or grease the tray with extra butter to stop the biscuits from sticking.

2 Cut the butter into smaller chunks and add into a mixing bowl. Add in the caster sugar and mix well until the two ingredients are smoothly combined.

3 Sieve in some of the plain flour and mix well; continue to add more of the flour and mix in until it has all been added and a thick dough has been created. Add in the Prosecco and vanilla extract and kneed the two liquids into the dough. If still quite dry, add another dash of Prosecco.

4 Separate the dough into four pieces and roll each one into a ball. Dust the work surface or chopping board with flour and use a rolling pin to roll each ball into a round, flat biscuit shape with fairly even thickness. Cook in the oven for 25 minutes.

Add in chocolate chips or other toppings of your choice.

Prosecco Apple Crumble

Ingredients

- **4 large cooking apples**
- **1 tbsp butter**
- **120ml/½ cup Prosecco**
- **1 tbsp brown sugar**

For the crumble
- **100g/3½ oz butter**
- **150g/5oz plain flour**
- **75g/3oz brown sugar**

Method

1 Pre-heat the oven to 170'C/325F/Gas3. Peel, core and cut the apples into small cubes.

2 Melt the butter in a pan on a medium to low heat before adding in the diced apple.

3 Gently stir for 2 to 3 minutes while the apple begins to soften. Pour in the Prosecco and add the sugar. Allow the apple to simmer for 2-3 minutes, stirring regularly to ensure the apple does not burn. Once the apple is softened and beginning to break up, take off the heat. Drain off some of the excess fluid and place in a baking dish.

4 To make the crumble add the butter, flour and sugar into a bowl. Use your index fingers and thumbs to rub these together to achieve a crumbly mixture. Add the crumble on top of the apple mixture and cover it well. Place in the oven for 25 – 30 minutes or until golden and piping hot

Prosecco Cocktails

Kir Royale

Ingredients

- **1 tbsp crème de cassis**
- **175ml/¾ cup Prosecco**

Method

1 Pour the creme de cassis into a wineglass.
2 Pour in the Prosecco and serve at once.

A simply delicious classic!

Candied Ginger Prosecco Fizz

Ingredients

- **6 pieces candied ginger**
- **200ml/1 bottle angostura bitters**
- **2 bottles Prosecco, chilled**

Method

1 Throw the ginger pieces into a small bowl and pour the angostura bitters over the top. Cover the bowl and leave at room temperature for about 4 hours.
2 Strain the ginger. Half each piece of ginger lengthwise and drop one half into the bottom of each Champagne flute. Top with Prosecco and serve at once.

Prosecco Bellini

Ingredients

- **60ml/¼ cup peach juice**
- **120ml/½ cup Prosecco**
- **Slice of fresh peach to garnish**

Method

1 Pour the peach juice into a Champagne flute. Slowly top with the Prosecco.

2 Cut a slit in the peach slice and hook it on the rim of the glass.

3 Serve and enjoy!

Lemon Prosecco

Ingredients

- **1 bottle Prosecco, chilled**
- **250ml/1 cup lemon liqueur, chilled**
- **Ice**
- **Handful blueberries**
- **To garnish:**
- **4 sprigs thyme**
- **½ lemon, sliced**

Method

1 Pour the Prosecco and lemon liqueur into a large jug and stir.

2 Drop a couple of blueberries into each glass. Add ice and fill with the lemon Prosecco.

3 Garnish each glass with thyme and a slice of lemon.

Campari & Prosecco

Ingredients

- **Ice**
- **120ml/½ cup Prosecco**
- **60ml/¼ cup Campari**
- **1 tbsp fresh grapefruit juice**
- **1 slice orange, to garnish**

Method

1 Fill your cocktail shaker with ice. Pour in the Prosecco, Campari and juice, and shake well.
2 Strain the mixture into a chilled Champagne flute or martini glass. Garnish with the orange slice and serve.

Watermelon Prosecco

Ingredients

- **1 watermelon**
- **1 bottle Prosecco**
- **4 sprigs fresh mint**

Method

1 Cut the watermelon into large chunks and remove the seeds.
2 Juice the watermelon chunks in a blender and strain.
3 Drop a watermelon star into each glass. Quarter fill the glasses with melon juice then slowly top up with Prosecco.
4 Add a sprig of mint to serve.

Elderflower & Gin

Ingredients

- **60ml/¼ cup elderflower cordial**
- **60ml/¼ cup gin**
- **1 bottle Prosecco, chilled**
- **4 sprigs mint**

Method

1 Mix the elderflower cordial and gin in a jug and divide the mixture between 4 glasses.
2 Fill each glass with Prosecco and garnish with a sprig of mint.
3 Serve and enjoy!

Raspberry Prosecco with Fig

Ingredients

- **2 tbsp raspberry syrup**
- **8 fresh raspberries**
- **2 fresh figs, thinly sliced**
- **1 bottle Prosecco, chilled**

Method

1 Drop one tablespoon of syrup into each of 2 chilled glasses.
2 Divide the raspberries and fig slices between the glasses, then fill each with Prosecco.
3 Serve at once.

For the best cocktail, make your own tasty raspberry syrup with equal quantities of sugar, water and fresh raspberries.

Lemon Fizz

Ingredients

- **1 tsp lemon sorbet**
- **Dash lime cordial**
- **250ml/1 cup Prosecco, chilled**
- **¼ slice lemon**

Method

1 Drop the lemon sorbet into a Champagne flute and splash a dash of lime cordial over it.
2 Top up with Prosecco, stir, and garnish with a slim quarter of a lemon slice.
3 Serve immediately.

Raspberry Lemon Prosecco

Ingredients

- **1 bottle Prosecco, chilled**
- **250ml/1 cup lemon liqueur, chilled**
- **125g/4oz fresh raspberries**
- **6 sprigs fresh mint**

Method

1 Pour the Prosecco and lemon liqueur into a large jug or pitcher, and stir.
2 Divide the raspberries and mint between 6 glasses, and pour the lemon Prosecco over the top.
3 Serve immediately.

Red Buck's Fizz

Ingredients

- **Juice of 1 blood orange**
- **120ml/½ cup Prosecco, chilled**
- **A few redcurrants, to garnish**

Method

1 Strain the orange juice, then pour into a Champagne flute. Top up with Prosecco.
2 Sprinkle on the redcurrants and serve at once.

A dramatic variation on the traditional Buck's Fizz!

Aperol Spritz

Ingredients

- **Ice**
- **120ml/½ cup Aperol**
- **120ml/½ cup Prosecco**
- **120ml/½ cup sparkling water**
- **1 slice fresh orange, to garnish**
- **1 slice fresh lime, to garnish**

Method

1 Drop ice into a large glass. Pour in the Aperol, Prosecco and water.
2 Stir, then garnish with a slice of orange and lime.
3 Serve immediately.

Floral Prosecco Cocktail

Ingredients

- 250ml/1 cup cold jasmine tea
- 1 tsp orange blossom honey
- 1½ tbsp elderflower cordial
- 1 grapefruit, juiced

- 60ml/¼ cup vodka
- Ice
- 1 bottle Prosecco

Method

1 Pour the jasmine tea into your cocktail shaker. Add the honey, elderflower cordial, grapefruit juice and vodka. Add ice to taste and shake well.

2 Strain the mixture into 4 tall glasses. Divide the Prosecco between the glasses, and serve immediately.

For an extra floral touch, try making ice cubes with edible rose petals or other edible flowers, and adding one to the bottom of each glass.

Plum Prosecco

Ingredients

- **2 plums, peeled and chopped**
- **4 sprigs thyme**
- **Juice from one lemon**
- **4 tbsp simple syrup**
- **Ice**
- **1 bottle Prosecco, chilled**

Method

1 Muddle the chopped plums with 2 sprigs of the thyme, lemon juice and simple syrup until all of the plum juices are released.

2 Pour the mixture into your cocktail shaker with ice and shake well.

3 Add crushed ice to 4 tall glasses and divide the fruit & syrup mixture between them. Top up with Prosecco

4 Garnish with the rest of the thyme. Serve and enjoy!

To make the cocktail even fruitier, add extra slices of plum to each glass.

Prosecco Sangria

Ingredients

- 500ml/2 cups mint syrup
- 1 bottle Prosecco, chilled
- 120ml/½ cup orange juice
- 1 lemon, zested, thinly sliced
- 1 lime, zested, thinly sliced
- 100g/3½oz fresh strawberries, sliced
- 6 fresh mint sprigs
- Crushed ice

Method

1 Pour the mint syrup into a large jug or pitcher. P

2 Add the Prosecco, orange juice, lemon & lime zest. Add the strawberries, the lemon & lime slices and the mint sprigs.

3 Fill 6 tall glasses with crushed ice. Pour the sangria over the top, and serve at once.

Fruity, refreshing, and always fun!

Prosecco Margaritas

Ingredients

- **120ml/½ cup tequila**
- **120ml/½ cup orange liqueur**
- **120ml/½ cup simple syrup, chilled**
- **120ml/½ cup fresh lime juice**

- **Coarse salt, to garnish**
- **1 bottle Prosecco, chilled**
- **Fresh lime wedges, to garnish**

Method

1 Pour the tequila, orange liqueur, syrup, and lime juice into a jug. Stir and chill in the fridge for at least two hours.

2 Run a lime wedge around the rims of 6 glasses, then dip the rims into a plate of coarse salt.

3 Add ice to the glasses and divide the chilled tequila mixture between them. Fill up each glass with Prosecco. Stir and serve with a lime wedge over the rim.

Adjust to taste by adding more tequila, lime juice or syrup.

Maple Fizz

Ingredients

- Ice
- 2 tsp maple syrup
- 60ml/¼ cup cranberry juice, chilled
- 120ml/½ cup Prosecco, chilled

Method

1 Half-fill your cocktail shaker with ice. Spoon in the maple syrup, then pour in the cranberry juice and shake well.
2 Strain the mixture into a tall glass. Top up with Prosecco and stir.
3 Serve and enjoy!

Simple Rose Prosecco

Ingredients

- 6 tbsp rose syrup
- 1 bottle Prosecco, chilled

Method

1 Pour 6 glasses of Prosecco, then drizzle a tablespoon of rose syrup down the inside of each glass so that the syrup slides down to the bottom.
2 Serve at once and enjoy!

Nectarini

Ingredients

- **1 bottle Prosecco**
- **3 nectarines, peeled, stoned, chopped**

Method

1 Chill 6 champagne glasses.
2 Meanwhile, sieve the nectarine pieces over a jug and push through all the liquid with a spoon.
3 Spoon a dollop of the nectarine puree into each chilled glass. Slowly top up with Prosecco.

Ginger Fizz

Ingredients

- **60ml/½ cup ginger wine/ginger liqueur**
- **1 lime, juiced**
- **½ bottle Prosecco, chilled**
- **Fine lime slices to garnish**

Method

1 Divide the ginger wine/liqueur and the lime juice between 3 Champagne flutes.
2 Top up with Prosecco. Stir gently and garnish with thin slices of lime.
3 Serve and enjoy!

If you prefer, you can use the syrup from a jar of stem ginger instead of ginger liqueur or wine.

Hot Toddy Cocktail

Ingredients

- 1 tbsp marmalade
- 1 tsp honey
- 1 clove

- Dash fresh orange juice
- Dash whisky liqueur
- 125ml/½ cup Prosecco, chilled

Method

1 In a small pan, gently heat together the marmalade, honey and clove. Once warm and combined, strain the liquid and leave to cool.

2 Once cool, pour the marmalade mixture into a glass. Splash in the orange and liqueur. Then top up with Prosecco.

3 Stir once and serve.

Warming and relaxing a on a winter's night.

Prosecco Mojitos

Ingredients

- 1½ limes, juiced, + ½ lime to garnish
- 2 handfuls ice
- 3 tbsp of caster sugar

- 60ml/¼ cup Bacardi
- ½ bottle Prosecco
- 2 sprigs mint

Method

1 Pour the lime juice, ice, Bacardi and sugar into a food processor. Pulse together until the ice is crushed.

2 Damp the rims of 2 cocktail glasses and dip them in caster sugar.

3 Divide the rum mixture evenly between the glasses.

4 Remove the mint leaves from the stems, tear them and drop half at the bottom of each glass.

5 Fill each glass up with Prosecco.

6 Garnish with a slice of lime on the rim and serve immediately.

A fabulous and fun alternative to the traditional mojito!

Damson Prosecco

Ingredients

- **60ml/¼ cup damson gin**
- **½ bottle Prosecco, chilled**

Method

1 Divide the damson gin between 3 champagne flutes and fill up each glass with Prosecco.
2 Serve and enjoy!

A delicious winter cocktail. Try with sloe gin instead of damson.

Pomegranate and Grapefruit Fizz

Ingredients

- **2 tbsp pomegranate juice**
- **2 tbsp grapefruit juice**
- **250ml/1 cup Prosecco**
- **1 grapefruit slice, to garnish**
- **Pomegranate seeds, to garnish**

Method

1 Pour the pomegranate and grapefruit juice into a tall glass and stir. Top up with Prosecco.
2 Garnish with a slice of fresh grapefruit and a few pomegranate seeds, and serve immediately.

Berry Bellini

Ingredients

- Ice
- 100g/3½oz strawberries
- 100g/3½oz raspberries
- 100g/3½oz blueberries
- 1 bottle Prosecco
- 120ml/½ cup vanilla simple syrup
- 175ml/¾ cup pineapple juice

Method

1 Throw a good handful of ice into your blender. Add all the other ingredients and pulse to the consistency you prefer.

2 Pour into Champagne glasses and serve at once.

Classic Prosecco Cocktail

Ingredients

- 1 cube sugar
- 5 drops Angostura bitters
- 2 tbsp brandy
- 1 bottle Prosecco, chilled
- 1 slice orange

Method

1 Drop the sugar cube into each flute and drizzle the bitters over the top. Allow the bitters to dissolve the sugar, then pour in the brandy.

2 Fill up with Prosecco and serve, garnished with an orange slice.

Strawberry Prosecco

Ingredients

- **120ml/½ cup Prosecco**
- **1 tbsp fresh orange juice**
- **1 tsp honey**
- **150g/5oz frozen whole strawberries**
- **Fresh strawberry or strawberry slices, to garnish**

Method

1 Blend together the Prosecco, orange juice, honey, and frozen strawberries until smooth.

2 Pour the mixture into a Champagne flute. Garnish with a whole fresh strawberry or strawberry slices. Serve and enjoy!

Rhubarb Bubbles

Ingredients

- **350g/12oz fresh rhubarb, finely sliced**
- **50g/2oz sugar**
- **2 tbsp water**
- **1 bottle Prosecco**

Sweet, tangy and fizzy, this is a perfect summer cocktail!

Method

1 In a small pan, heat together the rhubarb, sugar and water. Bring to the boil and simmer for 4 minutes or so, stirring occasionally.

2 Blend the rhubarb mixture into a smooth puree, and leave to cool.

3 When the puree is cold, divide it between six glasses. Top up each glass with Prosecco.

Lemon Sgroppino

Ingredients

- **3 tbsp limoncello, chilled**
- **1 scoop lemon sorbet**
- **250ml/1 cup Prosecco, chilled**
- **A few fresh mint leaves, to garnish**

Method

1 Blend together the limoncello, lemon sorbet and Prosecco until frothy.
2 Divide the mixture between 2 Champagne flutes. Garnish with fresh mint and serve immediately.

Blueberry Prosecco

Ingredients

- **125g/4oz sugar**
- **120ml/½ cup water**
- **200g/7oz fresh blueberries**
- **2 bottles Prosecco, chilled**

Method

1 In a pan bring the sugar, water and blueberries to the boil, Reduce the heat and simmer for 10 minutes. Set aside to cool.
2 When cooled, blend to a smooth puree, and strain into a jug.
3 Dollop a tablespoon of blueberry puree into each Champagne flute and top up with Prosecco. Stir gently and serve garnished with blueberries on cocktail sticks.

Clementine and Rosemary Prosecco

Ingredients

- **For the syrup:**
- **Handful fresh rosemary leaves, roughly chopped**
- **2 cups granulated sugar**
- **2 cups water**
- **Zest from 3 clementines**

- **For the cocktail:**
- **6 tbsp fresh clementine juice**
- **1 tbsp lime juice**
- **1 tbsp rosemary syrup**
- **½ bottle Prosecco**

Method

1 Make a rosemary syrup by heating the sugar and water in a pan, stirring occasionally until the sugar dissolves. Remove it from the heat and add the rosemary and zest. Stir, cover, and leave to cool. When it is cool, strain it into a jug or bowl.

2 Pour the lime juice, syrup, and clementine juice into a small jug and stir.

3 Pour the Prosecco into glasses and top up with the syrup mixture. Serve immediately.

Garnish with rosemary sprigs and a clementine slice.

Passionfruit Sangria

Ingredients

- **125g/4oz sugar**
- **120ml/½ cup water**
- **3 sprigs rosemary**
- **500ml/2 cups passionfruit juice**

- **2 passionfruits**
- **1 orange, cut into half slices**
- **1 apple, cored and sliced**
- **1 bottle Prosecco**

Method

1 Make a rosemary syrup by heating the sugar, water and rosemary together in a small pan. Bring the mixture to the boil and simmer for 2 minutes. Remove from the heat and leave to cool for half an hour.

2 Throw the orange and apple slices into a large jug. Scoop out the passionfruit and add to the jug.

3 Pour in the rosemary syrup, passionfruit juice and Prosecco. Refrigerate for 2 hours before serving.

For an even fruitier taste, mix everything together, except the Prosecco, the night before. Then add the Prosecco just before serving.

Prosecco Punch

Ingredients

- 100g/3½oz fresh pineapple, chopped into chunks
- 1 orange, thinly sliced
- 1 lemon, thinly sliced
- 1 bottle Prosecco

- 500ml/2 cups pineapple juice
- 250ml/1 cup orange juice
- 60ml/¼ cup lemon juice
- Sprigs of fresh mint

Method

1 Throw the pineapple chunks, and the orange and lemon slices into a large jug. Add a handful of mint sprigs.

2 Pour in the Prosecco and the pineapple, orange and lemon juices. Stir well.

3 Fill 6 wine glasses with ice and pour the punch over the top. If you like, garnish with another chunk of pineapple and a fresh sprig of mint. Serve immediately.

To get the most flavour from your mint, clap it between your hands before adding to the punch.

Blackberry Prosecco

Serves 6

Ingredients

- **150g/2oz blackberries, plus more to garnish**
- **60ml/¼ cup water**
- **50g/2oz sugar**
- **1 bottle Prosecco, chilled**
- **sprigs of thyme, to garnish**

Method

1 Heat the blackberries, water and sugar in a pan and bring to the boil. Reduce the heat and simmer for about 10 more minutes. Then strain the syrup into a bowl and allow to cool.

2 Drop 2 tablespoons of the syrup into each of 6 champagne glasses. Top up with Prosecco and garnish each glass with a sprig of thyme and 2 blackberries.

3 Serve at once and enjoy!

A colourful, light and refreshing cocktail for any occasion.

Sparkling Cherry

Ingredients

- **60ml/¼ cup cherry liqueur**
- **60ml/¼ cup Campari**
- **2 tsp cherry juice**
- **½ bottle Prosecco**
- **2 cherries**

Method

1 Divide the cherry liqueur and the Campari between 2 tall glasses. Add a teaspoon of cherry juice to each, then top up with Prosecco.

2 Garnish with a cherry in each glass.

Hawaiian Prosecco

Ingredients

- **60ml/¼ cup coconut rum**
- **120ml/½ cup pineapple juice, chilled**
- **½ bottle Prosecco, chilled**
- **2 slices fresh pineapple, to garnish**

Method

1 Divide the coconut rum and pineapple juice between 2 tall glasses.

2 Fill each glass up with Prosecco, and garnish with a slice of pineapple.

You may also enjoy....

A comical collection of quotes for prosecco princesses, wine aficionados and beer lovers.

In a world where moderation or even abstention of our favourite tipple has all but curbed our joy, we bring you a light hearted, comical collection of quotes, sayings, mantras and truisms that confirm what you already knew to be true.... that prosecco, wine & beer are good for you!